# Little Orphan ANNIE

and

# Little Orphan ANNIE
## in Cosmic City

# Little Orphan ANNIE

## and

# Little Orphan ANNIE in Cosmic City

## Harold Gray

DOVER PUBLICATIONS, INC., NEW YORK

Published in Canada by General Publishing Com-
pany, Ltd., 30 Lesmill Road, Don Mills, Toronto,
Ontario.
Published in the United Kingdom by Constable
and Company, Ltd., 10 Orange Street, London
WC 2.

This Dover edition, first published in 1974, is
an unabridged republication of the following two
books by Harold Gray:
*Little Orphan Annie,* as published by Cupples &
Leon Company, New York, in 1926.
*Little Orphan Annie in Cosmic City,* as published
by Cupples & Leon Company, New York, in 1933.
The works are reprinted by special arrangement
with The Chicago Tribune—N.Y. News Syndicate,
Inc.
The publisher wishes to acknowledge the co-
operation and participation of Mr. Herb Galewitz
as licensing agent for The Chicago Tribune-
N. Y. News Syndicate, Inc.

*International Standard Book Number: 0-486-23107-0*
*Library of Congress Catalog Card Number: 74-82198*

Manufactured in the United States of America
Dover Publications, Inc.
180 Varick Street
New York, N.Y. 10014

# Contents

---

# FOREWORD

Ladees an' Gentlemen, and all you young birds out there in front too;——

Un'customed as I am to public 'pearances, and all that alfalfa, I just want to say this bustin' into liter-chure is a big s'prise to me.

'Course I s'pose I ought to be sorta bashful 'bout having a swell pitcher-book like this put out all filled up with nothin' but fancy poses and wise cracks of yours truly. But you don't see me blushin', do you? No sir. Down where I come from you get over bein' bashful young. You gotta toot yer own horn or get run over. See?

Nope, I'm not bashful. But honest, folks, I'm proud, I am, that you and your relatives and neighbors, deep down in your hearts, thought enough of me to write in and ask to have a book like this put out.

Yessir, folks, it sure makes you feel swell to find out, sorta un's'pectedly, how many real true friends you have.

I thank you.

# HEARD IN PASSING

# WHEN WEALTH FLIES IN AT THE WINDOW

2

# PLANS FOR THE HOMECOMING

4

# THE SURPRISE

# MUSIC HATH CHARMS.

9

# THE LOST CHEE-ILD DISCOVERED

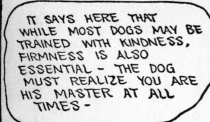

# SOME DROP

# TOO MUCH IS PLENTY

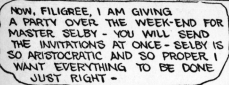

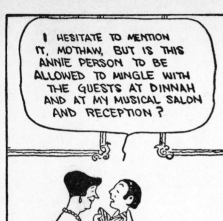

# SELF-DEFENSE

# THE BIG SHOW, BOYS!

# FIRST AID

# REPRISAL

# THE CHAMPIONSHIP STILL REMAINS IN AMERICA

# THAT FUNNY FEELING

# MAY TOMORROW NEVER COME

# BAD SIGNS

# THE APPROACHING HARVEST

# A SWEET CHARACTER

WHAT A LUCKY CHAP YOU ARE, WARBUCKS - A BEAUTIFUL WIFE, UNTOLD WEALTH, A HAPPY, WELL-APPOINTED HOME - A FORTUNATE FELLOW - YES A PERFECT ARRANGEMENT SAVE FOR THAT RATHER COMMON ORPHAN PERSON - I MUST CONFESS I CAN'T UNDERSTAND WHAT EVER INDUCED YOU TO —

WHAT'S THAT YOU SAID?

LISTEN, COUNT - NO OFFENSE, UNDERSTAND, BUT NO MORE SLAMS AT THAT KID, SEE? SURE SHE'S AN ORPHAN - WHAT OF IT? BUT SHE KNOWS ENOUGH TO KEEP HER NOSE OUT OF OTHER FOLK'S BUSINESS - GET ME?

THAT BIRD COMES THOUSANDS OF MILES JUST TO GYP ME - THAT'S FINE - I'VE BEEN TAKING CARE OF MY SCALP FOR YEARS AND HE WON'T GET IT - BUT ONE MORE CRACK LIKE THAT ABOUT MY ANNIE AND I'LL KNOCK HIS SCALP OFF FROM THE CHIN UP —

HAROLD GRAY

# TUT-TUT! CAN SUCH THINGS BE POSSIBLE?

# THE OLD FOX

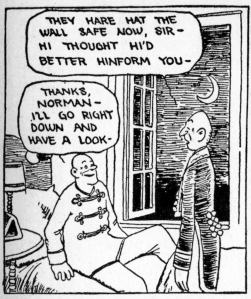

# THE BUSY COUNT

# A CLEAR CONSCIENCE

# CIRCUMSTANTIAL EVIDENCE

# THE MYSTERY SOLVED

# ANNIE'S LAMENT

# THE HYPNOTIST

# THE BAD NEWS

# RUBBING IT IN

# THAT DIRTY LOOK

# SMILE TODAY—WHILE YOU MAY

# EXPECTING THE WORST

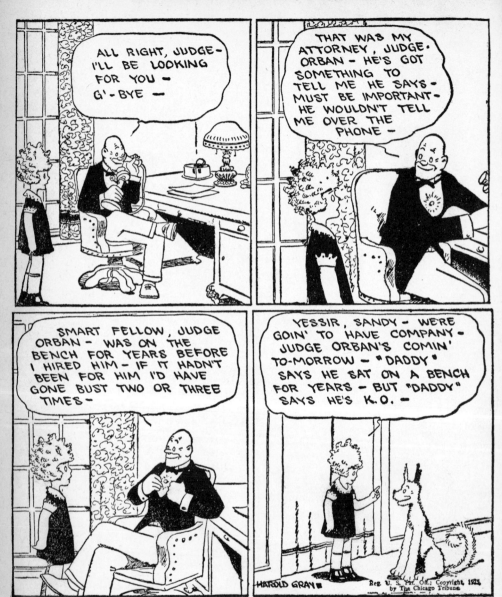

# THE JUDGE ARRIVES

63

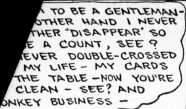

HAROLD GRAY

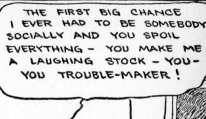

# HIS SHADOW

68

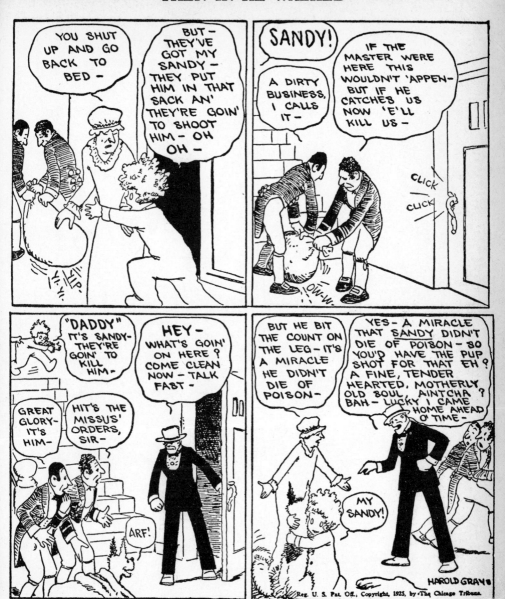

# THE FACE AT THE WINDOW

# RIGHT ON THE BUTTON

# WORD FROM THE DEPARTED

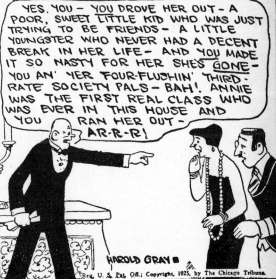

77

81

# HANDY SANDY

# FOUND

# DOWN ON THE FARM

# FOREWORD

THIS BUS is just leaving! Don't miss it, folks. See Cosmic City and the people in it. Rich Man, Poor Man, Beggar Man, Thief; Doctor, Lawyer, Merchant, Chief. All these and many more, including Mr. and Mrs. Futile.

We take you into their homes and behind the scenes, Folks. A trip you'll never forget.

Educational and Entertaining. Hurry, Folks! The bus is just leaving!

# NO-GOOD MONEY

# COSMIC CITY

# WELCOME, STRANGER

# PLEASED TO MEET YOU

# THE PARIAH

# A KINDLY MAN

# IN THE MIDDLE

# A GIRL OF ACTION

113

# STOP THIEF!

# TOM TAKE

YEP- TOM TAKE- SOME FOLKS CALL HIM A THIEF, I RECKON- BUT HE'S HARMLESS- LITTLE CRACKED, I FIGGER- DOESN'T REALLY <u>MEAN</u> TO STEAL- FOLKS LIKE HIM-

9-23-32

S'POSE I COULD ARREST HIM- BUT WHAT GOOD WOULD IT DO? DON'T AIM TO PUT FOLKS IN JAIL FOR THINGS THEY CAN'T HELP-

S'POSE A CHAP LIKE TOM TAKE IS O.K. WHEN YOU GET USED TO HIM- BUT LIVIN' NEIGHBORS TO A GUY, WHO PICKS UP THINGS AS EASY AS HE DOES, IS SORT OF A NEW IDEA TO GET USED TO-

WELL, IT SEEMS TO BE HERE, ALL RIGHT- BUT I'LL NOT FEEL SAFE 'TILL I FIND A BETTER PLACE TO HIDE IT- "DADDY" GAVE ME A PRETTY GOOD ROLL 'FORE HE LEFT- I'D HATE TO LOSE IT-

HAROLD GRAY

9-26-32

GEE- THEY'RE ALL BUSTED UP-
AND WHO WOULDN'T BE?
'MAGINE KNOWIN' YOU'RE GOIN'
TO LOSE YOUR HOME IN JUST
FIVE DAYS, WITHOUT A CHANCE
O' SAVIN' IT-

YESSIR- OLD
PINCHPENNY IS GOIN'
TO FORECLOSE- HE
DOESN'T NEED TH'
HOUSE- HE'S JUST
NATURALLY MEAN, THAT'S
ALL- PLEADIN' WITH
HIM WOULD BE A
WASTE O' TIME- BUT
SOMETHIN' MUST BE
DONE-

HAROLD
GRAY

# NOT MAD—ONLY ANGRY

# WHAT WILL THE MORROW BRING

I HATE TO HELP THAT OLD SKINFLINT, BUT IT'S THE LAW AND I'VE GOT TO SERVE THESE PAPERS- AND TOMORROW I'VE GOT TO ASK YOU FOLKS TO MOVE OUT-

PA AND I HAVE LIVED HERE EVER SINCE WE WERE MARRIED- IT'LL BE HARD TO LEAVE THE OLD PLACE-

IT'S THE LAW- I RECKON THERE ISN'T A THING WE CAN DO, BUT GET OUT-

9-30-32

FIVE HUNDRED AND FORTY-SEVEN DOLLARS- GEE- I'VE GOT IT FROM THE DOUGH DADDY GAVE ME- BUT IF I GIVE IT TO 'EM, SO THEY CAN KEEP THEIR HOME, I'LL BE BROKE- AS IT IS, I CAN CHECK OUT ANY TIME AND FIND A NEW HOME- THERE GOES THAT OLD BUZZARD NOW- LOOK, SANDY- SEE HIM?

GR-R-R-

WELL, EVERYTHING IS WORKING OUT AS I WISH- IT ALWAYS DOES- I'LL SHOW PEOPLE IN COSMIC CITY THAT IT'S NOT HEALTHY TO OPPOSE ME- LET 'EM THINK OF ME WHAT THEY WILL- I'M WITHIN MY RIGHTS-

IT'D SURE BE ROTTEN BUSINESS TO SPEND IT THAT WAY- IT'D LEAVE ME LESS'N A BUCK- BUT TH' FUTILES HAVE BEEN SWELL TO ME- COURSE, IT'S NOT HAVIN' MONEY THAT COUNTS; IT'S WHAT YOU USE IT FOR- BUT, JUST TH' SAME, IT'S NICE TO HAVE, TOO- AND IT'D PAY MY CAR-FARE BACK TO THE CITY AND FRIENDS-

HAROLD GRAY

# THE PAYOFF

Panel 1: AHEM— WELL, YOU'VE HAD YOUR NOTICE— OF COURSE YOU'RE NOT ABLE TO PAY $547, OR ANY PART OF IT, SO OUT YOU GO— IT'LL DO YOU NO GOOD TO BEG— I'VE BEEN MORE THAN EASY WITH YOU— CONSTABLE, DO YOU DUTY—

10-1-32

Panel 2: JUST A MINUTE, YOU CHEAP, SMALL-TOWN CHISELER— THERE'S YOUR MEASLY FIVE HUNDRED AND FORTY-SEVEN BUCKS— COUNT IT—

B-BUT WHAT'S THIS? I THOUGHT—

Panel 3: YOU DO JUST WHAT SHE SAYS AND DO IT QUICK—

WHO CARES WHAT YOU THOUGHT— HEY, YOU FOLKS— YOU'RE WITNESSES— NOW YOU HAND OVER THAT MORTGAGE AND SCRAM— THERE'S THE DOOR—

Reg. U. S. Pat. Off.; Copyright, 1932, by The Chicago Tribune.

Panel 4: GET OUT— AND IF I EVER CATCH YOU SETTIN' FOOT ON THIS PLACE AGAIN, I'LL SET MY DOG ON YUH—

HAROLD GRAY

124

# SO IT'S TO BE WAR, EH?

125

# THE PERFECT ALIBI

126

# SHARING HIS LUCK

127

# HIS MASTER'S VOICE

# OPPORTUNITY KNOCKS

# IN THESE DAYS A JOB'S A JOB

134

# HER CHAMPION

# FIRE AND BRIMSTONE

# KNOWLEDGE IS POWER

138

# OVERHEARD

WELL, I GOT ALL THE "COURIERS" DELIVERED IN A HURRY TODAY— THIS JOB'S A CINCH, AS SOON AS YUH GET YER ROUTE FIGGERED OUT AND KNOW WHO GETS PAPERS— AND THE PAY IS GOOD, TOO—

11-4-32

BUT, MOTHER, IT ISN'T RIGHT— ANNIE PAID OFF THE MORTGAGE ON OUR HOME— AND NOW IT'S WHAT SHE EARNS THAT BUYS MOST OF WHAT WE EAT— MY PENSION IS SO SMALL—

WHY CAN'T I FIND A JOB? I WANT TO WORK— BUT NO ONE WILL HIRE ME— THERE SEEMS TO BE NO PLACE FOR ME— I CAN'T STAND THIS IDLENESS—

GEE— I DIDN'T MEAN TO EAVESDROP— POOR MR. FUTILE-SHUX— I'M GLAD TO HELP 'EM OUT ALL I CAN— THEY GAVE ME A HOME, DIDN'T THEY? I'LL TIP-TOE BACK TO THE GATE AND THEN WHISTLE AND WALK LOUD WHEN I COME IN— HE MUSTN'T KNOW I HEARD—

HAROLD GRAY

# THE PROBLEM

# THE GOOD EARTH

# WHAT A MAN

# PROGRESS

# THE INDIRECT APPROACH

150

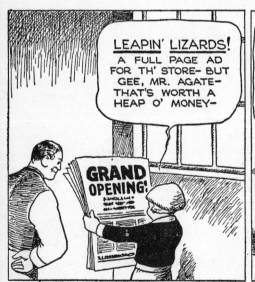

# GRAND OPENING

# THE MENACE

# A HANDY MEMORY

# ISN'T THAT JUST TOO BAD

# CAN SUCH THINGS BE?

WHEE- C'MON SANDY- LET'S PRETEND I'M A TRAPPER IN TH' NORTH WOODS AND THIS IS A BLIZZARD- GEE, WE'VE NEVER BEEN UP ON THIS HILL BEFORE- WE'RE OVER A MILE FROM TOWN-

12-8-32

OH, LOOKIE, SANDY- THERE'S A LITTLE HOUSE DOWN THERE- I NEVER KNEW ANYBODY LIVED UP IN THESE WOODS- AWFUL POOR LOOKIN' PLACE- WONDER WHO LIVES HERE-

NOW, I TELL YE, SELINA, I'M AGOIN' FER TH' DOCTOR- YOU'VE BEEN LAID UP FER A WEEK AND YOU AIN'T GETTIN' A BIT BETTER-

BUT, ZEKE; WE AIN'T GOT A CENT TO PAY NO DOCTOR- AND IF WE HAD, TH' CHILDREN NEED FOOD-

LET ME GO FOR TH' DOCTOR, PAW- I KNOW TH' WAY-

AW, YOU AIN'T GOT SHOES-

LEAPIN' LIZARDS! WHY, I DIDN'T S'POSE THERE WAS ANYBODY SO POOR AS THOSE FOLKS- THEY HAVEN'T GOT ANYTHING- TH' KIDS ARE BAREFOOT AND IN THIS WEATHER- AND THEY'VE GOT SICKNESS- GEE-

HAROLD GRAY

# HELPING THE HELPLESS

# THE SPIRIT OF CHRISTMAS

169

171

# INVENTORY

# LOOKING BACKWARD

NO NEWS IN TH' PAPER— NOTHIN' SPECIAL EVER SEEMS TO HAPPEN 'TWEEN CHRISTMAS AND NEW YEAR— GUESS EVERYBODY IS GETTIN' OVER CHRISTMAS AND SORT O' WAITIN' FOR 1933 'FORE THEY START ANYTHING—

12-27-32

WELL, THIS WEEK IS A GOOD TIME TO GET YER SECOND WIND AND LOOK BACK OVER WHAT'S HAPPENED TH' PAST YEAR— I'VE HAD A FEW CLOSE SHAVES, BUT EVERYTHING HAS WORKED OUT O.K. FOR SANDY AND ME—

WONDER HOW THAT MEAN MISS TREAT IS MAKIN' OUT THESE DAYS— AND WHERE ARE "DADDY" AND TRIXIE NOW? AND HOW ARE JAKE AND BILL AND WUN WEY AND DOC LENS—

'SPOSE I COULD WRITE A LETTER TO JAKE OR MAW GREEN— BUT THEY THINK I'M IN A GIRLS' SCHOOL— I'D HAVE TO 'S'PLAIN— THEY'RE NOT WORRYIN' AND I'M ALL RIGHT— WHY GET EVER'BODY ALL 'CITED?

HAROLD GRAY

# A MIND FOR BUSINESS

# HAPPY DAYS ARE HERE AGAIN

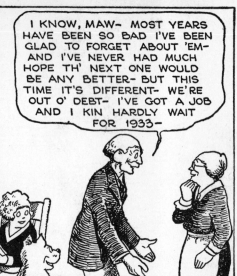